Thoughts of Poetry

By:

Keith Gerald Smith

ISBN-10:0692699562
ISBN-13:9780692699560

CONTENTS

DEDICATION

This book is dedicated to my wife, who had the
foresight to guide me to the publication of my poetry.

CHAPTER 1:

Love

Meeting You

Meeting you for the first time
Representing myself like I should
Failing to be myself like I could
Introducing to you all the things I want to be
Creating a façade for only you can see
All these things I want you to believe
It's only false prophets, it's only conceit
Who am I, someone who cheats, still or kill
Who am I, someone who teach the will to feel
The emotions that are hidden, the pain that is given
I continue to anticipate meeting you for the first time.

Understanding Me

You don't understand me
Falling in love with you, and not creating a bond
You don't understand me
Putting up with the pain you caused
You don't understand me
Blaming me for things I have not done
You don't understand me
Stressing me out, making excuses for you ways
You don't understand me
Hoping that there may be better days
You don't understand me
Trying to satisfy your needs
You don't understand me
Praying that one day you'll see what I see
You don't understand me
You Don't understand Me
You don't Understand me
Just Try to understand Me

You

Missing you is like stabbing myself
Missing you is like grabbing myself
Thinking about the positive things
Things that made sense at the time
Now you purposely created these signs
These signs that was interrupted with grief
Caused lots of pain that confused you with relief
Yea, it was me, right, that hurt your little heart
Yea, it was me that took it, loved it, and tore it apart
With all these flaws that you said I had
It never occurred to you that I was really sad
Sad inside my soul, creating a bond for you to hold
But it's was me, me that put up with your flaws
Ignored all these laws, laws of love that any human wouldn't
stand
Yet stayed to work on this tragic in hand
Yea, I know it was me, it was me
Sh--------t, it was you, you caused your pain
It was you, who should be to blame
Blamed for your loveless ways, your passionless days
Days that I discovered were full of false hope
Hope that I thought was realistic yet, turned as a joke
Yea, it was you, you, you............................

Love Signs

My love for you seems complicated at times
Never satisfied with the message you carry in these signs
These signs are flashed; leave, stop, stay go away
Confuses me with the sense of building up my wall
The emotional boundary doesn't mean I love you less at all
It does capture the exhaustion of stubbornness
Delaying a constant view of your feelings
Help me understand you to understand me

It's Over

Who are you, telling me that it's over
Conducting a painful feeling in my heart
Making me feel guilty about my part
My part was giving you things I never shared
Like my love, in my past it was never spared
I was trying to compromise with all this pain
This pain, you didn't realize was driving me insane
Making me think about the negative experiences
I know my past hunts me with no restrictions
Creating this boundary that caused my convictions
You'll probably never understand why these words are so strong
Making me think my emotions are wrong
Time after time we've been through this scenario
If I give you what you want I may weep what I sew
Don't use this leverage to force my hand
Fooling yourself like you're making a stand
You're about to lose me lady, you don't even see
I guess you don't know how much you mean to me
I think you should take this in, or maybe carry on with your life
I wanted to pack up my shit many times, yet I stuck out the fight
I'm not making excuses about these hunting emotions
No matter what you think I gave love and devotion
So it's over, that's what you said
This so called relationship was full of life, now it's dead

Sadness & Hope

I'm conducting myself to think about the good things
The good things we shared, the feelings that was spared
Many times I felt threatened of your kindness
Disturb with your independence and unselfish ways
Yet, I'm conducting myself to think about the good times
Confused about my feelings for you, too late for this thought
Continue to stress on your independence creating a doubt
A doubt on us, wondering could it be repaired, our love that is
Could this be the end of a love that had a promising future
Yet torn over the years with unsettled battles of trust
Years of blame, years of the same selfish games
I can't explain this pain I feel, this is a disturbed life I live
If I could do it again and had a choice to regain a change
I could say I would, yet it probably would stay the same
I'm not perfect; I'm not a specialist in this field of love
This field is definitely complicated yet, I'm still here
I'm here because I wanted to be here, now you're leaving
Leave with the knowledge of me loving you
I'm conducting myself to think about the good things

Lust

A pretty woman can take the patience of a man
A pretty woman can take the pride of a man
A pretty woman can arrive to her peak
Staying in control of her posture
Qualifying her figure with that sense of glare
That sense of glare, that man's eye
That qualification of her smell, her touch
The touch is the ingredient that blends
Blends so well with that connection
That connection creates a bond around the heart
You what? Love me. Love me for what
For my sensitive style, I'm not in denial
Love you back, you're confused
Supporting your own rules
You don't love me, haven't even paid dues
I'll holla, holla from a distance
Get the message you're non-existent
In the back of my mind
I'm collecting a creative sign, Wooooooooo
I can't go on it's done
Yet, I did have fun, until worst became to none

Love

Loving you is like a treasure that I cherish
Letting you in my room of distant gloom
Creating these things that are so dear to me
Such as your smile that captivates a chill
A chill that I simply feel as you touch me
That touch carries the message to my heart
Orchestrated vibes that answer the Questions
Do you love me, do you want me, how, why
Answer with a smile and it concludes instantly

CHAPTER 2:

TRUTH

Conducting A Message

Trapped in this jungle with these Lions
Staying away from their eyes of prey
Being weary of the tactics they may create
The focus is on the freedom that's given
Not mentioning the emotions that's driven
With the fear of what these lions may produce
Keeping a likable interest trying to confuse
Stay away from these evil beasts
If you know what's good for you
This is a message that valued ones should hear
Collect this information without a sign of fear
Come into the light and experience this journey
This journey, this journey that is so complicated
Once captured, once stripped, so often duplicated
Over the years we surrender our words yet not our souls
Constantly degrading, always hesitating
Never get old, always been told, this story
It being called his story, his story, O history

Truth

She was so beautiful years ago
Had a colorful look about herself
She had remarkable curves that was unexplainable
Not mentioning her spirit that captured the essence
The essence was the qualification that she has presence
Presence, her presence, full of courage, full of pride
Pride that was not questioned by any
She raised her own with ethnicity
Built a culture of strong unselfish breeds
Created a tribe that conducted skills to live
The rain, the pain, the shame, there's blame
The soul of her nature tortured and killed
Disable lain without a will
Murder, murder
That's what it's called

Reflection

Don't hate me cause you ain't me
All the things you want to see
Like me dead or slaving for free
Creating this hate on your own
Knowing the pain that was caused was definitely wrong
Who you hate, me, cause I figured you out
You should've known it was coming, without a doubt
Look now, times have changed
I've invented all these important things
I'm a doctor, lawyer, extraordinaire
Conducted many rallies and demonstrations
So my own could travel anywhere
I've followed through with the athleticism
Using strengths of my mind and body as a mechanism
So don't hate me cause you ain't me

Triumph

Smothering myself with these emotions I feel
Keeping a note in my mind that maybe it will fade
Fade to what, I ask myself, adding that same note
That note of confusion about my life, where am I
Hoping a change will conduct itself with a purpose
Scared of failing or of disappointment, I am acknowledging
Acknowledging the soul effort I put to perform
Yet, I discover it may not be enough to satisfy greatly
I do alert myself I am blessed with this presence of health
Not taking for granted the purpose of love for my family
I am confused at times that this may be what I am
I am confused at times that this may be who I am
I continue to conduct myself with spiritual energy
Let me find my way and help me along the way
Not demanding these efforts yet asking for some relief
Relieve me from this emotional roller coaster
Capture my mind to expand of a traveler's thought
Convince me that this will pass and I will come up
The light I know I will find, yet I know it will shine
I have faith it will shine in my direction

A Painful Past

Karma collects a victory in my life
Carrying the pain of joy with a smile
Defeating the confused heart with an instant blow
Creating its' message continuously and abruptly
This monster is here maintaining its' ground
Engraving a mark of intense emotion through confusion
Confusion that is understood only through the pain
That pain that was mentioned, what goes around.....
You follow that right, comes around
That karma is created I guess for a reason
That reason to create that burden of pain
It insists to strike at that moment of weakness
It is here now continuously destroying the heart
That heart is a simple measure that pain travels through
That karma is labeled the substance of all vengeful things

The Game

Making a light note of this delightful potion
Creating this specimen with a sizing observation
Coming into the den of challenging players
Playing by their rules yet, thinking that yours are stale
These amazing rules may destroy you instantly
Continuing this battle of unfamiliar players
This games is crucial with all these new rules that are set
The game begins with a little deceitfulness
It hits you suddenly that the rules are the same
Crumbling by the way side, fierce blow to the heart
Forcing the conclusion that the game and the rules never changed
The players continue to never remain the same
You still got it, breaking it down, making them fall
Making them fall constantly to their knees, that is
Yes, yes, the game remains the same

Untitled

Explaining these thoughts complicates its possible meaning

CHAPTER 3:

FAITH

From the Lord

No, you can't help me
My help comes from the Lord
The Lord helps me lift my spirits to a higher ground
He provides me with the faith that I live for
He is real, he is connected with ones who believe
Lord, thank you for life, thank you for choices
Lord, thank you for the voices you share
I am grateful for everything you've given me
I am blessed with the ability to do what I do
So, Lord, thank you for guiding me
There's no other, you're all I need
No, you can't help me
My help comes from the Lord

Come Lord

I am struggling right now thinking about this wall
This wall that I run into when I'm leveling my speed
Knowing in my mind that he will come
I'm anxious about his presence that he creates
Craving that thought that everything will be alright
Believing in his word yet, needing an awareness
Knowing in my mind that he will come
Come Lord and find your way into my mind
Comfort me Lord, create calmness in my heart
Come to me Lord, make my worries vanish
Come to me Lord, ease my pain
Knowing in my mind that he will come
Give me that strength in knowledge of my enemies
Guide me over the wall that denies my level of speed
Let me find my interest of calling and perfect the value
Grateful I am, blessed with all these things
Knowing in my mind that he will come

In God's Hands

The Lord collects gifts from this life
He brings peace within pain
He gives joyful knowledge
He creates an atmosphere of care
The Lord collected another gift of life
That gift was a special one
A gift that touched everyone that knew her
Lady you were a wonderful creation made
Thanks for the experiences and knowledge
Thanks for those special moments of humor
The Lord collected another gift of life
That gift shined with a bright sparkle
That sparkled glared through many
Thank you for being my friend
God bless you Dorothy Toomer

Faith

In this room these walls are closing in ever so fast
Study creating this suffocating method
This method is draining energy from my thought
Coping with the short breaths that I am taking
Entering a heated sweat of exhaustion
Reaching out to the ceiling of clouds
Waiting for a door to open so quickly
Rescue me from this awful setting
Yet, I do hear noise outside this room
This noise is giving me strength to live
Wait patiently, I hear, I shall be rescued
Come to me, come to me, I will wait
This message has given me another breath
This message is life; life is this gift of faith
Faith opens this door and creates happiness

ABOUT THE AUTHOR

Keith Gerald Smith lives a quiet life in a small Florida town. He is a beloved husband, father, son, and friend. Keith has dedicated his life to the betterment of mankind through committed service to people in need.

www.ingramcontent.com/pod-product-compliance
Lightning Source LLC
Chambersburg PA
CBHW022352040426
42449CB00006B/841